Creative Paper Design

 NEW YORK **Reinhold Publishing Corporation**

Published in the United States of America 1961
by Reinhold Publishing Corporation
Library of Congress Catalog Number 60-16591
Printed in Holland

Reprinted, 1962

CONTENTS

This book is addressed to all who realise what pleasure there is in creating. It is not only written for teachers or the so-called talented, but particularly for the timid, who feel the urge to draw and paint, but are too modest to believe in their faculties.

The much-abused term 'art' has therefore been avoided. All the illustrations show the work of pupils in schools or training courses, or of first-year college students. The work produced by these different groups can stand comparison in regard to skill and inventiveness. This proves that everybody of no more than average talent is able to create. The author does not share the opinion of many teachers and psychologists, who hold that the child's considerable gifts in this field die with the beginning of adolescence. I have found in over thirty years' experience that imagination and creativeness stay alive throughout adolescence. Unfortunately, however, these qualities can be killed by bad examples and the wrong kind of teaching. In as much as young people are usually encouraged to imitate the work of adults, they lose faith in their own ability and their healthy relationship to the material. Most education appeals primarily to the intellect, and a natural development of the creative faculties is therefore thwarted. The original, living imagination of the adolescent is choked with scientific and literary concepts and as result, he only rarely develops an understanding for the art of his time. It is easy enough to achieve results with children who are still unspoilt. They still have a genuine relationship to the material, can still 'feel' it with all their senses and only need slight encouragement.

By contrast, adolescents and adults are inhibited, because they have too many examples before them, and set themselves too high a standard. To regain their creative faculties, they must rid themselves of all rigid concepts and established standards, and try to re-discover the delight in tools and materials, in discovery and inventiveness.

It is the purpose of this series to help towards this end. The author is fully aware that books of this kind have their danger: the examples shown can be only too readily imitated, if they are not properly understood, instead of serving as a source of inspiration. But it is hoped that the illustrations show the origin and metamorphosis of various shapes so clearly, that the student can follow them quite easily and will achieve entirely original results.

Ernst Röttger

5

The child's natural urge to play takes two distinct forms: aimless play, which leads merely to tears and quarrels; and serious play, which always follows a pattern of some kind even though the child may not be aware of it. In the informal, improvised dances of children, for instance, a definite rhythm can be clearly distinguished.

All real play follows certain rules. This also applies if we play with creative media. Medium and method are determined by these rules, and it is through them that the game acquires purpose. Another characteristic of real play is the absence of utilitarian ends. No one knows what the result is going to be; it may cause surprise, give joy or turn out to be quite dull. It is the truly liberating activity of the game that counts, and not the results.

The term 'play' is not used in the visual arts. And yet, the methods of leading artists of our time show that 'play' also has its justification in sculpture and painting. In contrast to the sculptors and painters of the last century, who based their work on certain rigid concepts and considered material only as something very subordinate, some of today's greatest artists regard material as a source of inspiration. They can thus discover new forms of expression, almost as if in play.

What are the creative elements? First, the materials used; second, the forms of expression: dot, line, area, three-dimensional shapes, space and colour; and finally, the principles that give unity to the whole.

The following chapters show some of the things that can be made in the course of such play, working along certain lines. The pictures can tell far more than words, and explanations have therefore been kept to the absolute minimum.

Key to the captions

V = made in the training course of the Werkakademie, Cassel

L = the work of adults and students at teachers' training courses

M = the work of a child (girl)

J = the work of a child (boy)

The small numbers give the age

All the examples shown in this book were made in classes held by Ernst Röttger and Dieter Klante. All the photographs were taken by Dieter Klante.

Splitting an area into sections

The task: an area is to be cut up into several portions, and these are to be brought into a new rhythmically balanced relationship.

The rules: these are determined by material, basic form, the number of cuts, the run of the cuts (straight or curved, horizontal, vertical or diagonal), the retention of the original form or its transformation.

Severe limitations will make good results all the more likely.

It is advisable to use at first only black cardboard against a white background, to cut only in one direction, and to keep to straight or curved lines only. In later exercises, different shapes and lines can be used together.

There is one basic rule for all exercises: Nothing must be added or taken away.

When a satisfactory solution has been found, the pieces are pasted down.

Figures 1—3 show the simplest ways of splitting-up

1

2

3

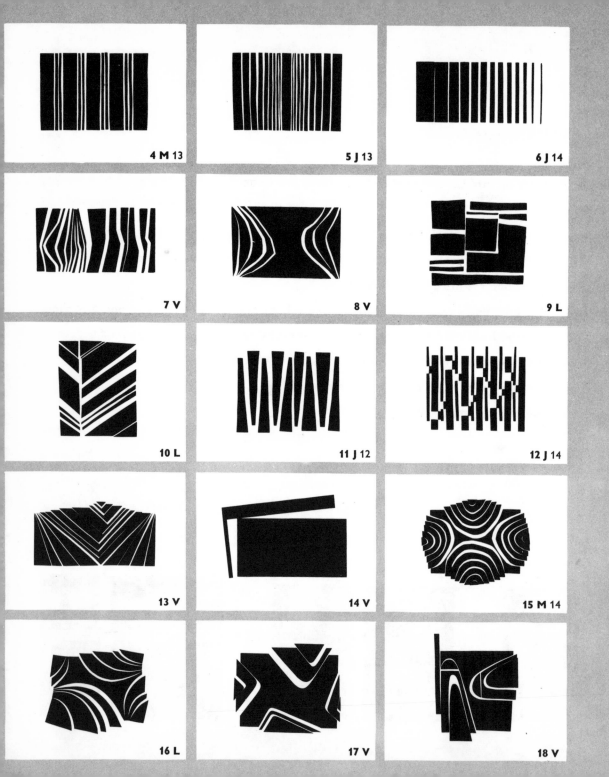

4 M 13

5 J 13

6 J 14

7 V

8 V

9 L

10 L

11 J 12

12 J 14

13 V

14 V

15 M 14

16 L

17 V

18 V

STARTING FROM THE RECTANGLE

Figures 4-18: a few ways of transforming a rectangle by splitting-up. Examples 4, 5 and 6 were produced according to the same rule, which allows only vertical division. The form of the rectangle had to be retained.

The aims were:

Figure 4: a balanced rhythm of equal parts

Figure 5: movement, intensified towards the middle

Figure 6: movement in one direction

Figure 7: introducing movement through broken lines

Figure 8: establishing a balanced relationship through curved lines on both sides

Figure 9: splitting-up through horizontal and vertical cuts

Figure 10: division through one horizontal and several diagonal cuts

Figures 11-18: transformation of the area by cutting in different directions. The basic form has been changed. It should be borne in mind that these illustrations are on a greatly reduced scale. It is advisable to use a rectangle at least eight to twelve inches long for the first exercises

Figure 19: Division according to a rule demanding a build-up around three circular areas (the grain of wood, a whirlpool, etc.)

Figure 20: Division where the area could only be cut into on one side. The resultant shapes were to be moved out and brought into a harmonious relationship. (There is a strong pictorial effect, in contrast to the earlier examples)

Figure 21: this example is reproduced full-size. It shows particularly well how the technique of splitting-up can lead to textile or marquetry design. It is the work of a housewife

19 L

20 V

12

21 L

22 V 23 V 24 V 25 V 26 V 27 V 28 V

STARTING FROM THE TRIANGLE

Figures 22-7: a sampling of the infinitely varied possibilities

Figure 28: it seems hardly possible that the basic form was an equilateral triangle

Figure 29: a striking three-dimensional effect

14

29 V

30

31

32

33

34

STARTING FROM THE CIRCLE

The form of the circle is full of promise. The examples show clearly the rules followed each time.

The following tasks have proved very rewarding in the class-room:

At least ten circles of equal size are cut out from dark cardboard or stiff paper (about 4 ins. diam.). Each area is to be split up according to different rules, and re-arranged to form a related whole. Practised pupils can be asked to do as many as fifty different schemes. The best solutions, selected on the basis of good proportion, are then repeated on a larger or smaller scale, according to the characteristics of the work. All the examples shown on page 17 have been developed from the circle, whose form can be restored by making the pieces fit into each other

35 V

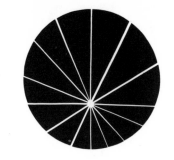

36 V

37 V

38 V

39 V

40 V

41 V

42 V

43 V

WAYS OF SPLITTING UP

A mask has to be developed out of a basic form (square, circle, oval, triangle . . .) by cutting the latter in a manner determined by the rules of the game. The resultant parts are to be arranged until a certain expression has been achieved. These experiments are particularly thrilling for children, since the smallest change will produce quite a different expression.

Here, too, the basic rule is most important: never add or take away.

Natural forms can be used as well as geometric ones, as in figures 50-2, which are based on the outline of a fish.

Plant forms, too, are eminently suitable (leaves, buds, blossoms, trees, etc.).

In figures 54-6 and 62 the paper has been torn instead of cut. It can be seen that the line achieved by tearing is more suitable for natural forms than a straight cut.

Differently coloured papers can also be used. Example: two pieces of paper of equal size, and of the same basic shape, are placed on top of each other and cut up together. This will produce two differently coloured pieces of new shape. These can be transposed, or arranged in layers of different colours. After a few repeated successes, papers of several colours, or even patterned papers, can be used.

44 V

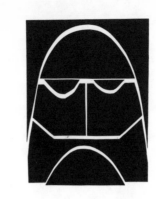

45 V

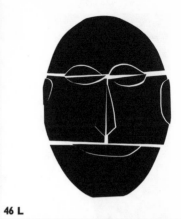

46 L

47 V

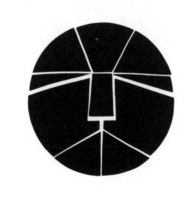

48 V

49 V

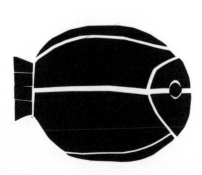

50 J 12

51 L

52 V

53 V

An impressive poster-like effect, illustrating the suitability of this technique for poster design (greatly reduced in scale).

54 V

55 V

56 V

57 M 12

58 V

59 V

60 J 12

61 L

62 V

63

Cutting out and folding back

The following exercises require paper that is black on both sides.

Figure 63 shows how to proceed.

The rules determine the basic form, the shape of the areas to be cut out, their size and number, and the choice of material (colour and type of paper).

Here, too, it is advisable to start with black and white paper. Only simple forms are cut out and folded back at first. When the pupil has gained some experience, he can gradually be allowed more freedom. He can then use other kinds of paper (with a different colour on each side, or, perhaps, with patterns) and a greater variety of shapes, not necessarily of the same size. But choice and arrangement of forms and colours will continue to be governed by certain rules (contrast, patterns of movement, etc.).

Figures 64-80 merely hint at a wealth of possibilities.

Basic rule: nothing must be taken away or added.

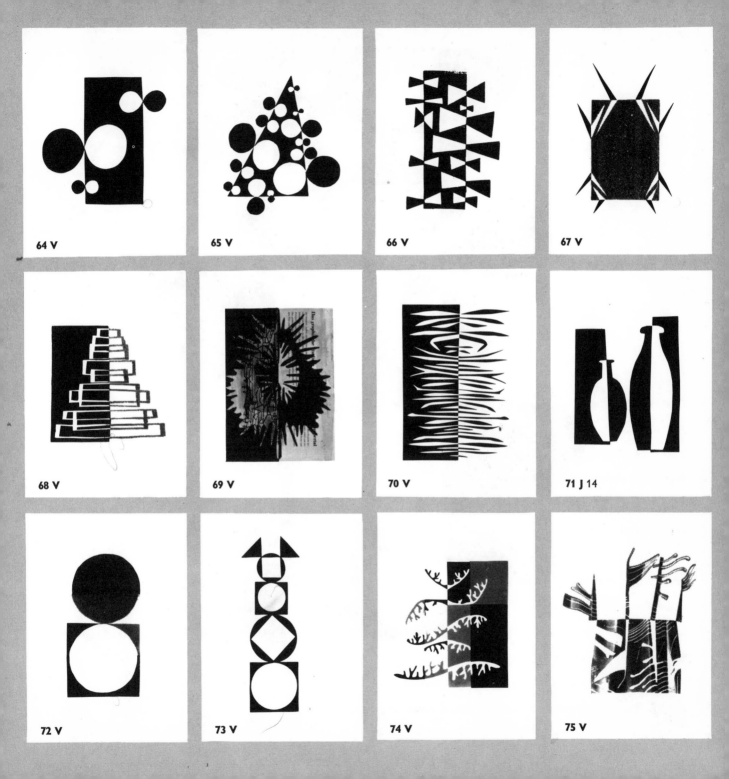

64 V

65 V

66 V

67 V

68 V

69 V

70 V

71 J 14

72 V

73 V

74 V

75 V

76 V

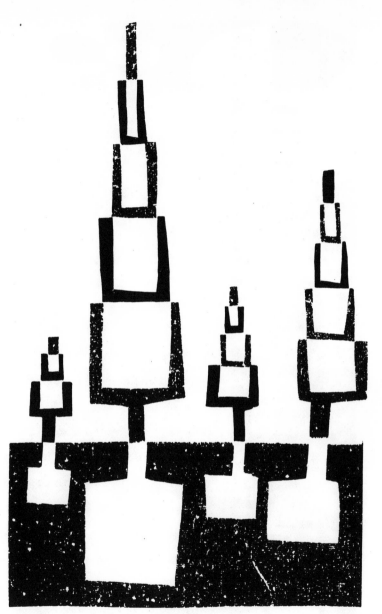

77 V

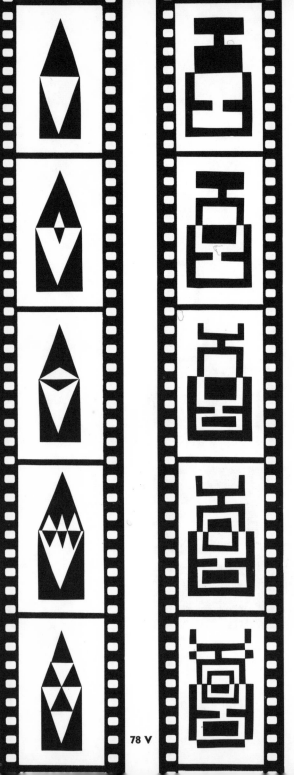

Figures 78-9 show the different phases of a game. Tasks which demand the development of certain forms in stages can be particularly fruitful. There is but one step from here to the slow motion picture.

A young student — who had been trained in Sweden — showed a film he had made of experiments of this kind. It was supported by sound effects, which brought the process of opening out and folding back very much to life. The film could not have impressed the audience more if it had been a series of slow-motion pictures of formative processes in nature and one suddenly realised how close a game of this kind comes to recapturing natural metamorphosis and decline.

Figure 80: variations on the triangle

FURTHER POSSIBILITIES

Having carried out the previous tasks successfully, and having derived pleasure from them, the pupil will soon want to experiment on his own.

In the examples shown in figures 81-4, splitting up and folding out have been combined.

Figures 85-8 show other possibilities

Here, the cut-out shapes have been placed next to each other, producing a surprisingly strong rhythmic effect.

If different kinds of paper are used in these exercises (rough against smooth, glossy against matt, striped against mottled, pure against dull colours, etc.) the dramatic quality can be heightened, and pictures can even be produced.

Here, again, the author would like to point to the possibility of applying these results to textile design, appliqué work and marquetry.

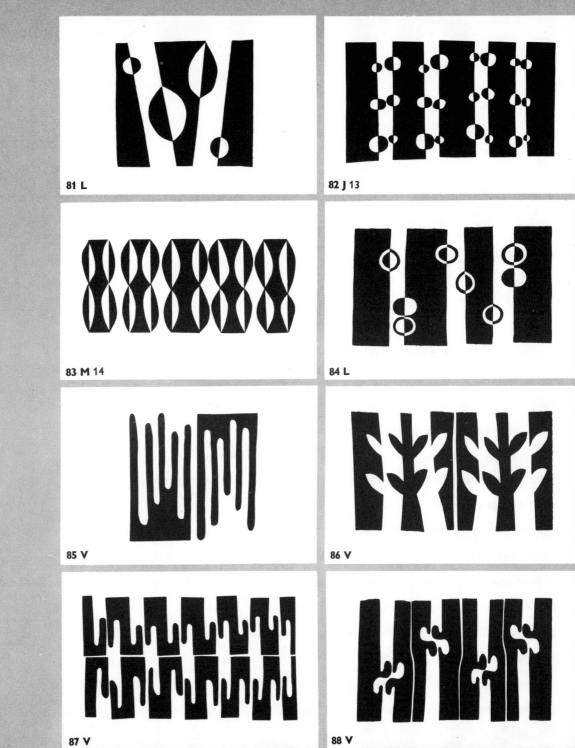

81 L

82 J 13

83 M 14

84 L

85 V

86 V

87 V

88 V

Transformation by folding

Paper of every kind can be used for this purpose, as long as it is to some degree transparent. Tissue paper can be placed against a black background, having first been folded. This will give it the quality of a delicate veil. The task: to divide an area into regions of grey by folding.

Basic shape, and number and run of the folds are determined by rules.

Again: nothing must be added or taken away.

It is advisable to work against a larger, double sheet of transparent paper, so that the results can be checked at each stage by holding the double sheet against the light. If the final result is satisfactory, the paper can be pasted down in one or two corners (paste must be used very sparingly in work of this kind, because it is apt to leave marks).

Figures 89-95: starting from a square

Figure 96: starting from a circle

Figure 97: starting from a triangle

It is only after, with the entire uncut area, that we start with cutting out and re-arranging individual shapes.

89 V

90 M 13

91 M 12

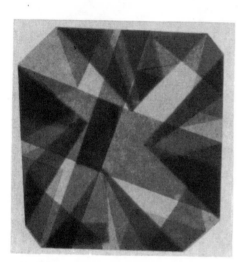

92 J 14

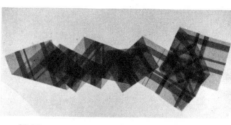

93 V

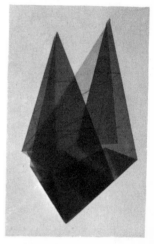

94 V

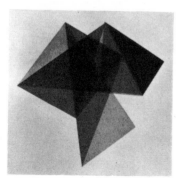

95 V

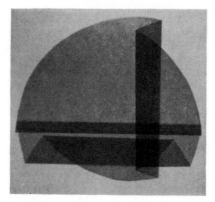

96 V

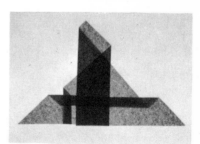

97 V

98   99   100   101   102

103 V

104 J 12

105 V

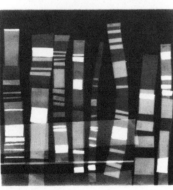

106 V

Figures 98-102: ways of folding strips of paper

Figures 103-8: here, the task was to group strips of paper

Figure 103: two tapered strips of paper, folded to produce a straight and a curved line respectively

Figures 104-5: two strips of equàl width, folded at a right angle, placed on top of each other at a right angle

Figure 106: a particularly striking arrangement of strips of different width, folded several times in places

Figures 107-8: arrangement of torn strips

Note: Figures 103, 106, 110 and 116 are reproductions of negatives. The forms therefore appear dark where they should be light and vice versa

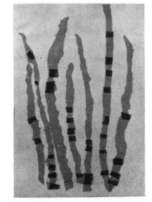

107 V

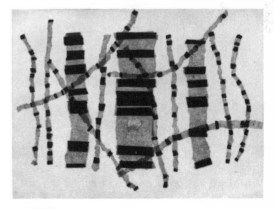

108 V

109 V

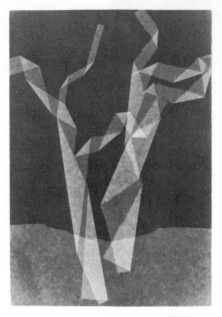

110 L

111 M 14

USING STRIPS OF PAPER

Figure 109: a branch

Figure 110: trees

Figure 111: flower and butterfly

Figures 112-19: transformation of a rectangle (figure 117: transformation of a circle) through cutting into and folding back at right angles

Figure 115: another example based on the rectangle, which, in this case, has only been cut into at a right angle on one side, rather like a comb. The strips have also been folded at right angles only

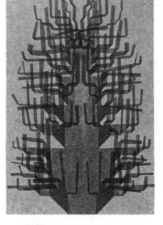

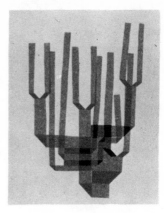

112 J 13   113 V   114 V

115 V

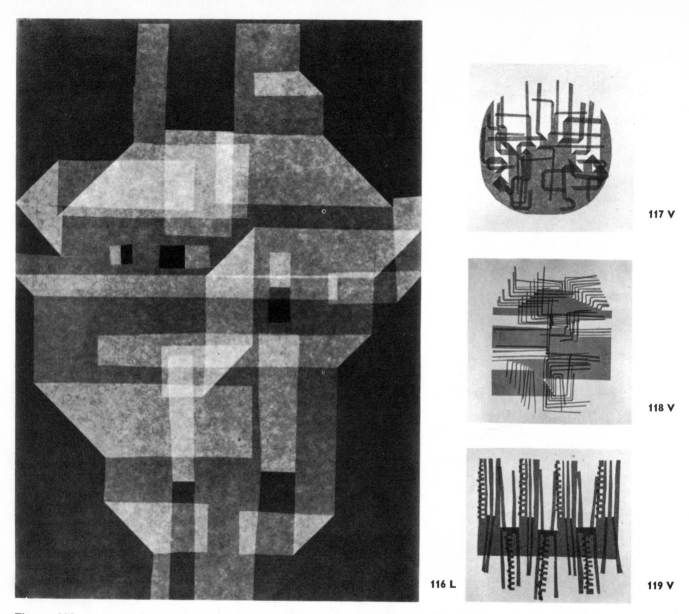

117 V

118 V

116 L

119 V

Figure 116: a rectangle, cut into at a right angle and folded. Some of the shapes are the product of folding outwards

Figure 120: breaking up a square by cutting into at right angles and folding. (used as design for a tapestry, replacing the shades of grey with colours)

121 M 15

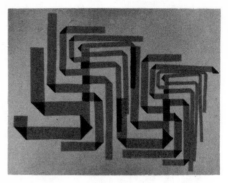

122 V

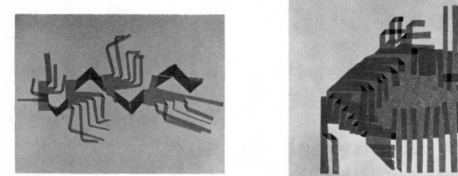

123 V

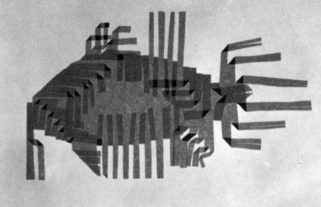

124 V

Figure 121: dividing an area by folding horizontally and opening out and folding back some squares

Figures 122-3: further break-up of the original area

Figure 124: the outline of a fish was drawn on a square piece of paper, and cuts could only be made as far as the fish, at a right angle. The strips were then folded, producing the effect shown in the illustration

Figures 125-6: grouping forms within the given area

38

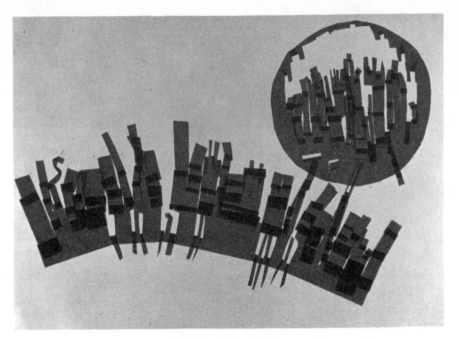

125 V

126 V

Veiling

Further effects can be achieved by placing layers of paper on top of each other. Indeed, coloured transparent papers lend themselves to unlimited possibilities. Here, too, deliberate restriction of technique and firm rules are advisable.

It is best to start with two layers, advancing step by step to more. This also applies to the use of colour. Since colour is an additional factor, its function, in this case, must be clearly defined. (Already in working with two colours, it should be stated whether there should be sharp contrasts, or merely dark-light, clear-opaque, warm-cold, etc., effects).

After the student has produced several satisfactory examples in one or two colours, the rules can be somewhat relaxed to admit others.

Tissue paper will prove particularly suitable in colour work.

If torn paper only is employed (plate I), form will take second place. To strengthen the feeling for colour, torn papers alone should therefore be used at first. By contrast, the pupil should do further exercises of this kind with cut-out shapes only, fiishing by using both cut and torn pieces.

Figures 127-8: several layers of torn paper. The strips (figure 127) have been folded in several places

Figure 129: layers of cut and torn paper. Separate parts are based on geometric forms (triangles for the sails. rectangles for the masts, and a variant of the trapezium for the hull). The circle has been cut out of the mount

A fine example of children's work

Pieces of coloured tissue paper, torn and arranged in layers to form a tree. A good example of the use of pure and mixed colours

Plate I

Pieces of coloured tissue paper torn out, cut, folded and made to form a flower. The veiling effect, obtained by arranging the paper in flat layers, can be further accentuated by inserting coloured transparent papers

Plate II

A fish, made of pieces of cut transparent paper. Since it would seem rather isolated against its background, vertical strips of coloured paper were added. A lively and original example, made by a student of little experience

Plate III

127 L

128 L

129 J 14

130 J 14

131 L

132 V

133 V

134 V

Relating forms within an area by cutting and folding back

A form is cut into a sheet of paper with a razor blade, a knife or stencil cutters, and folded back. The task consists in arranging this shape in some definite relationship all over the area of the sheet. Whether the shapes have to be of identical or different sizes is determined by the rules. To start with, it is better to keep to one size. The illustrations show that this limitation has produced particularly good results.

Figure 143: a strong three-dimensional effect

135 V **136 V** **137 V** **138 V**

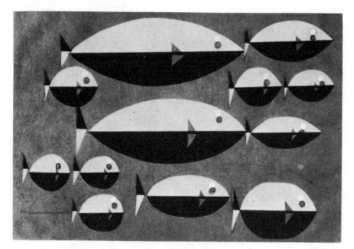

139 V **140 M** 13 **141 M** 14

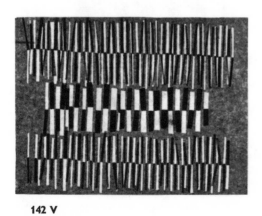

142 V **143 V**

144 J 13

44

145 L

These photographs are full size. This type of work almost demands the largest possible scale. Its possible application to textile and marquetry design is obvious

Cutting out and folding back can also be done over several layers. The more layers we use, the greater the variety of tones of grey.

It is best to make the transition from layer to layer rather gradual, using at first the same motif. The examples on page 47 show how this could be done.

The project 'a group of houses' was at first to be carried out over one layer (figure 146), then over two (figure 147), and finally over three (figure 148), always excluding the mount.

Note how few shapes have been used. In the case of three layers, only rectangles were cut out and folded back. Pages 48 and 49 show various other methods.

Figure 149: an insect, developed out of the rectangle by cutting into and folding

Figure 150: silhouette of a bird, built-up in triangles

Figure 151: a mixture of organic and geometric forms holds the elements of great tension (birds and triangles). Some portions were cut out and pasted down

Figure 152: trees, folded and then cut out, are placed on a sheet of paper and partly put on top of each other Only very little folding has been used in places to heighten the effect

Figure 153: using three layers. Almost a pictorial effect, because of the free use of shades of grey

146 J 12

147 L

148 M 14

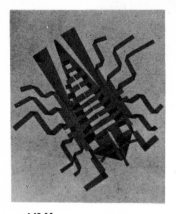

149 V

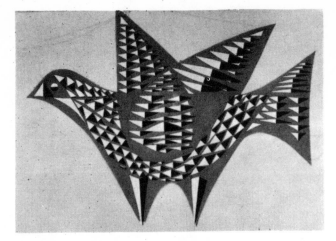

150 V

151 V

48

152 V

153 V

154 L

The following examples are the work of adults and are in no way less original than those shown on the previous pages — proof, surely, that the right method can bring the creative faculty back to life.

Figures 154-5: the wings of the insects are partly cut out of the mount. They were put back, though in a slightly changed position. All the other portions are added (folded, or in layers)

Figure 156: three layers. Repeated folding has created a highly sculptural effect. The houses are the result of cutting and folding, the trees cut out and replaced at a slight angle. Nothing has been added

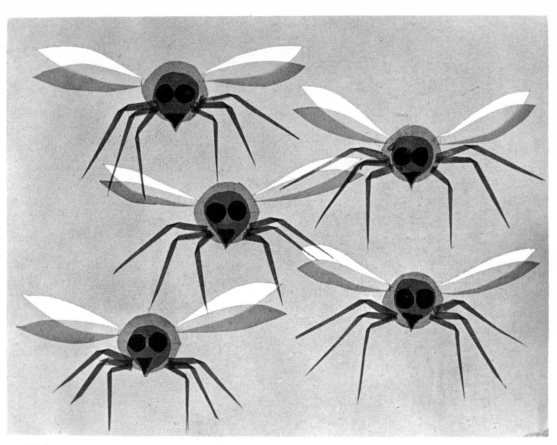

155 L

156

It will be obvious, from the examples shown so far, that a combination of techniques offers almost unlimited possibilities. But the teacher must do the exercises himself, because it is only through practical experience that the incredible scope of games with paper and other materials can be fully appreciated. Above all, such experience will bring home the importance of deliberate restriction to material and technique.

Obviously, this is not art, but merely creative play for amateurs, and has to be judged accordingly. The criterion will be the arrangement of colours and shapes according to certain rules, both in abstract and more realistic themes. It is the aim of this series to help discover the laws underlying the creation of a work of art, and thus to gain an understanding of art itself.

The illustrations on pages 53-6 and 57 merely show the development of earlier techniques

52

157 V

158 V

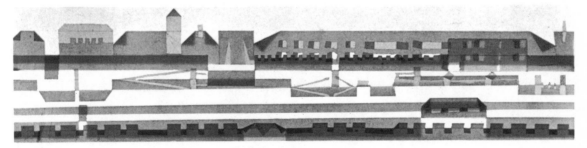

159 V

160 L   161 L

Figures 160-1 show the division and transformation of a rectangle. A rectangular piece of transparent paper has been divided into three rectangles and folded into three layers. Several large rectangles with rounded corners were cut out of the uppermost layer, a smaller number of smaller rectangles out of the middle layer, and even fewer, quite small ones, out of the last.

Figure 160 shows the work unfolded, top layer on the right, bottom layer on the left.

This game can also be played with the paper folded several times, or only twice.

Further examples are shown in figures 163-4 and 166-8.

The number of layers of paper, as well as number and size of the shapes to be cut out or torn, is laid down at the start. There is no need to keep to purely geometric forms.

Again, the game can be varied by using layers of coloured transparent papers.

Figure 162: the task was to replace the cut-out shapes elsewhere on the sheet. The author would like to point to the possibilities of reproducing such work by various photographic techniques. Transparencies are particularly suitable for shadow plays.

54

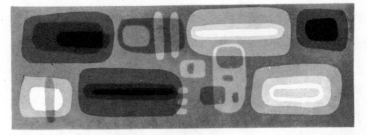

162 L

163 L

164 V

166 V

167 V

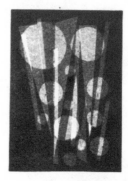

168 V

165 V

Figure 165: using crumpled tissue paper

56

169 V

170 V

171 V

172 V

Figures 169-72: the areas were cut out of three layers

A design for a window, created in this manner, is more convincing than one produced on a drawing board.

Designs of this kind can also be made three-dimensional by translating shades of grey into relief (plaster, wood, glass, or slate)

Relief

As in the previous exercises, a surface is to be brought to life by cutting into it, except that the cut-out forms are not folded down. The illustrations on the next page show that even a multiplication of identical forms can produce quite a striking plastic effect.

Note the importance of light in this type of work. In each case, light must be treated as an important component. The scope of the game is considerably widened by including light. The photographs in this volume have tried to bring out this aspect. The examples have been shown in the 'proper light', i.e. they were lit up to bring out their special qualities as much as possible.

The most suitable material, in this case, is white drawing paper. Coloured paper is not recommended, because colour does not admit subtle degrees of light and shade, although there is no objection against the use of metal foil.

It is left to the reader to retrace the stages of the examples in figures 173-90

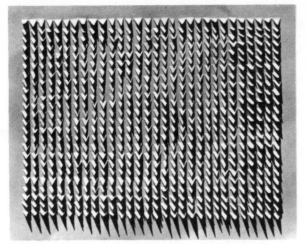

173 J 12

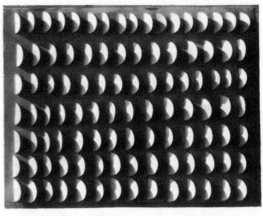

174 M 12

175 V

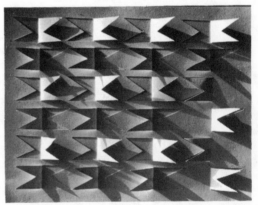

176 V

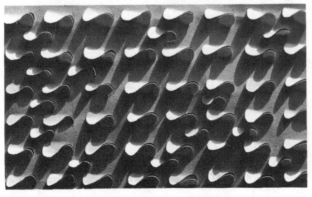

177 V

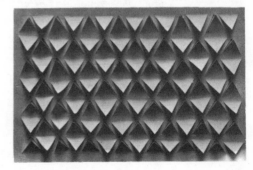

178 V

179 **J** 13

180 J 14

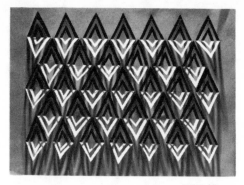

182 J 13

181 M 14

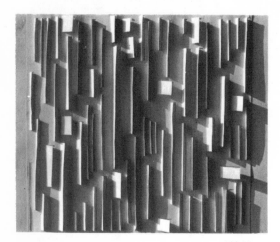

183 V

184 V

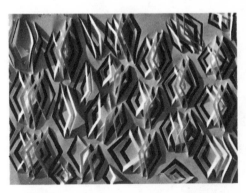

185 V

186 V

187 V

188 M 13

189 V

190 V

191 J 14

192 V

193 L

194 J 12

195 J 12

196 V

197 V

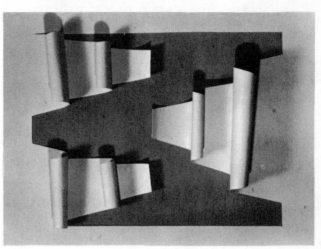

198 V

Figures 191-2: natural forms in relief

Figures 193-4: the forms, cut into and raised almost at a right angle, are standing upright. Children can build a whole city, a factory, or a forest in this manner

Figures 197-8: the forms were rolled outwards and drawn through slits

Relief on drawing paper, made by cutting into and folding out. Nothing has been added or removed

199 V

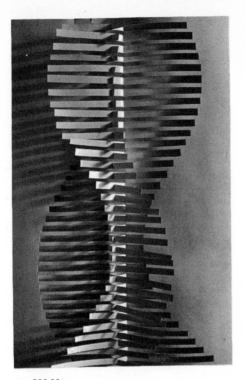

200 V

201 V

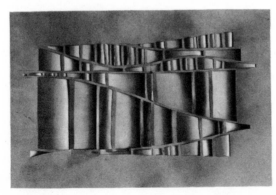

202 V

203 V

RELIEF BY INSERTING STRIPS OF PAPER

The task: A sheet of paper is to be brought to life by cuts, through which strips of paper are to be inserted, forming a definite pattern.

The rules determine whether the strips are to be cut or torn, and if they are to be of the same or different width or of a certain shape.

Figure. 204: a loose, informal effect, created by torn strips

Figure 205: plaiting with strips, which have been pasted down

Figure. 206: a severely geometric arrangement

Figure 207: diagonal slits. The strips were given one twist before being inserted

Figure 208: diagonal slits. A lively rhythm has been created by not letting all the strips rise to the same height above the surface

Figure 209: strips of paper were twisted into cords and pulled through narrow slits on both sides, thus appearing alternately in full length and in small sections

Figure 210: still a relief in character. Strips of equal size were inserted through slits made in a folded sheet of paper

204 V

205 V

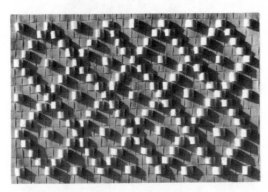

206 M 15

207 V

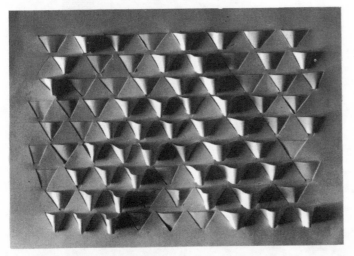

208 V

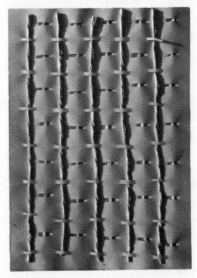

209 V

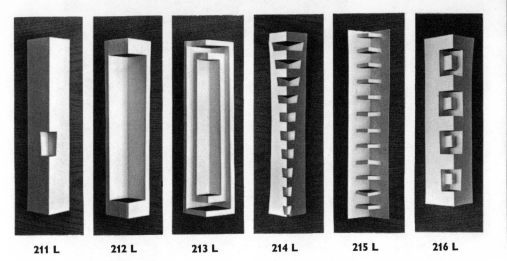

211 L   212 L   213 L   214 L   215 L   216 L

217 L

THE TRANSITION TO FREE SCULPTURE

Figures 211-16: narrow rectangles are folded lengthways and are cut into at right angles along the crease. The forms are then pressed in (when using cardboard, mark with a knife before folding).

These examples form the transition from the relief to free sculpture. It is advisable to make several objects of different size, and to compare them for their plastic effect. The next step leads to making rectangular bodies (drawing paper).

The aim is to achieve a form of balanced rhythm

218 L

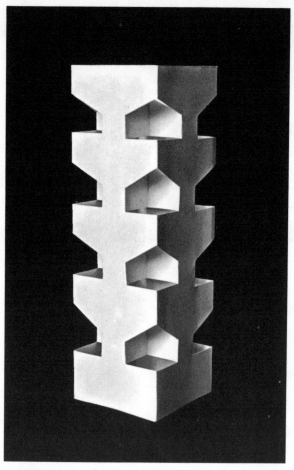

219 L

Figures 218-19: a rectangular piece of paper has been folded into a body with a square base (remember that the paper has to be pasted together at one edge!). This form was built up by cutting into and pressing in along the edges

Figure 220: a similar procedure, applied to a body with a hexagonal base

Figure 222: a dramatic effect, obtained by making cuts of varying width and depth

Figure 221: a simple square block made more interesting by working a strip of paper round it

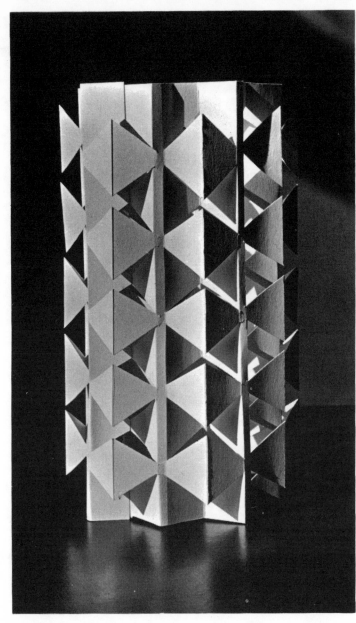

220 L

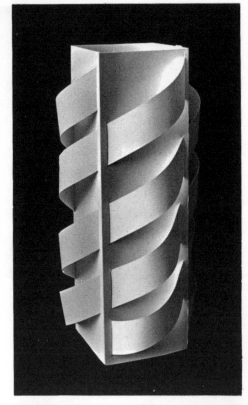

221 L

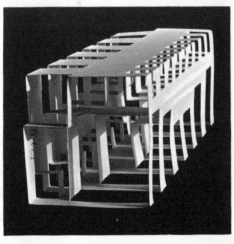

222 L

75

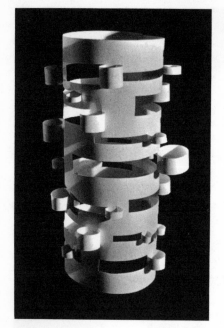 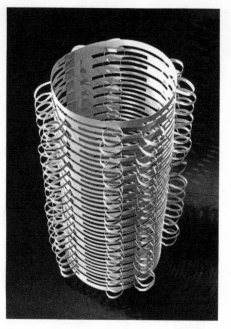 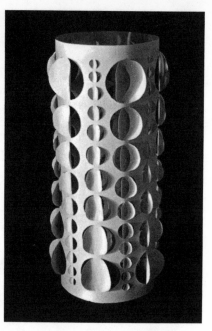

223 J 13   224 V   225 V

HOLLOW CYLINDERS

The two edges of a piece of drawing paper are joined to form a cylinder, first cutting into it forms, which are folded back, rolled, or pressed in. Details are determined by rules.

It might also be suggested that the edges be joined without paste, as in figures 224-5 and 227-8

Figure 229: emphasis on structure. The run of the ribs gives this cylinder great strength

Figure 231: cylinder with vertical slits. Height and width can be varied indefinitely by pressing down or pulling out

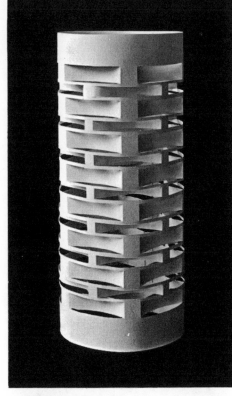

226 L

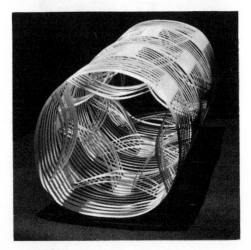

227 V

228 V

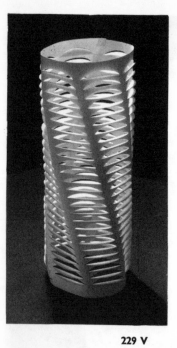

229 V

230 V

231 L

232 V

233 V

234 V

Figures 232-3, 235: completely new forms have been achieved by creasing. Truly an invitation to the inventive!

Figure 234: strips, pulled out of a piece of rolled paper, are joined at the top with a circular lid

Figure 236: again a variation of the cylinder whose shape has been made less severe by pulling in the upper and lower edges with strips of paper

The examples shown on pages 76-79 can inspire a whole series of lanterns, etc. Whole columns of lit-up cylinders can be constructed for garden parties, etc. It is advisable to use an inner cylinder of transparent paper where the outer walls have been pierced to any extent.

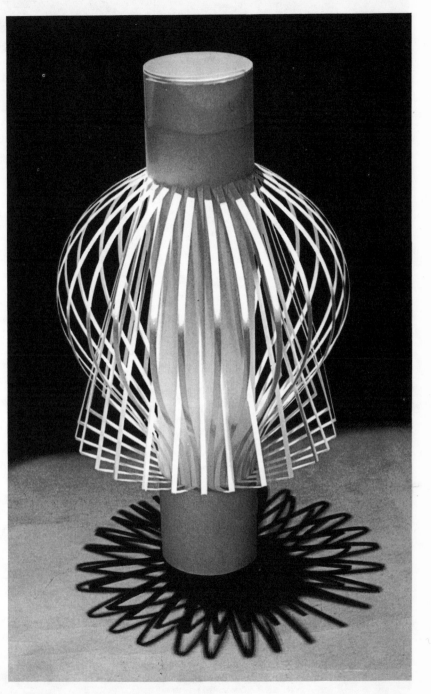

235 V

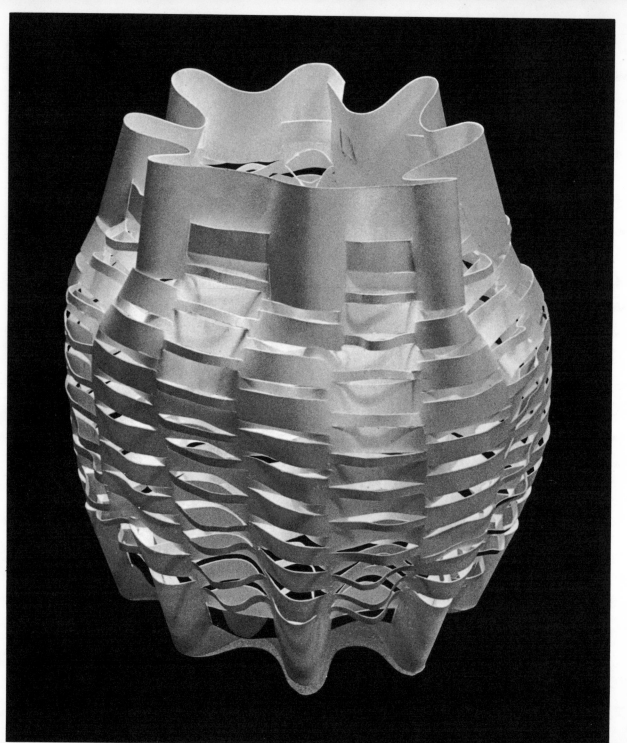

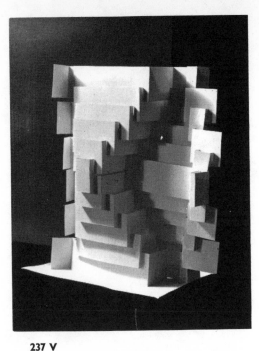

237 V

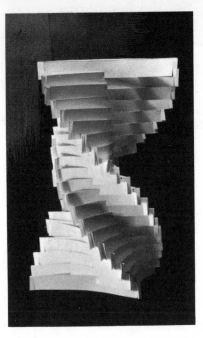

238 V

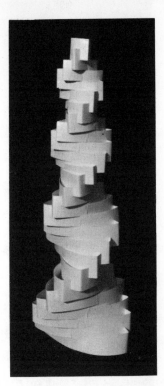

239 V

Building

WORKING WITH STRIPS OF CARDBOARD

Cut out strips of cardboard. The task is to cut into these strips up to half their width, and to join them at these points, thus forming structures without the use of glue or paste.

It is advisable to start with strips of equal width, and to make the transition to strips of varying width very gradual.

The strips can also be folded at right angles or combined to simple forms, which are then used for building. Here, too, it is most important to keep within clearly defined limitations.

BUILDING WITH FOLDED PAPER STRIPS

Strips are cut out of white paper (writing paper, tracing paper or drawing paper) and folded lengthways to form right angles (mark line with a knife when using drawing paper).

Number, length and width of paper strips, as well as the type of building, are laid down by the rules of the game. Some tasks might be 'upward movement', 'overhanging upper storeys over a small base', 'horizontal over a vertical base', a 'rhythmic arrangement of forms of two, three or more sizes'.

The strips must be cleanly joined with a little paste.

The link between projects of this kind and building in metal is obvious. The structural elements—angle irons, T-bars (obtained by joining two angle irons), steel joists, etc.—are the same for both.

Almost anything can be made, from simple buildings to machines in working order. The illustrations on page 83 suggest some possibilities.

Tasks of this kind are also very suitable for teamwork, each set of parts being entrusted to a group of students. This can be a useful discipline in craftsmanship and accuracy, because bad work is likely to be rejected by other members of the group.

Figure 241: a simple, well-proportioned structure

Figure 245: giant wheel, rotated by a simple weight-and-roller mechanism (the roller is also made of paper or cardboard)

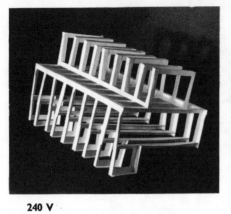

240 V

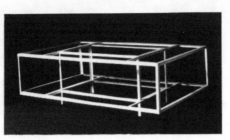

241 V

242 V

243 L

244 V

245 L

246 L

Figure 246: scaffolding with inset coloured panels

84

247 J 14

A machine with a difference: for once not the symbol of utilitarianism, but a toy with no function but to give pleasure. Today, children are very mechanically minded. The construction of a machine of this kind is a particularly suitable task for the adolescent; by stimulating inventiveness, attention is diverted from an adult interest in usefulness and profit.

The machine shown above was thought out and built by a fourteen-year-old boy.

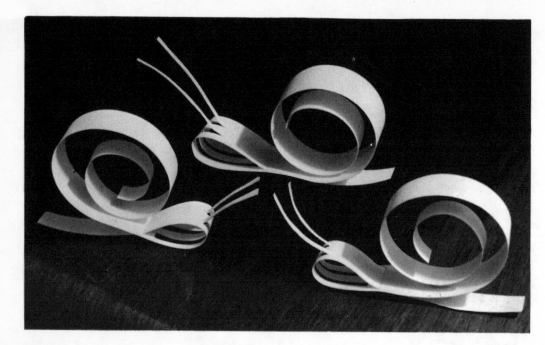

248 L

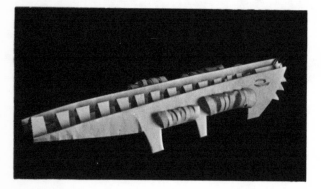

249 V

250 L

251 J 14

Natural forms

Figures 248-50: how to develop natural forms from basic components. These creatures must be made without adding, taking away, or using mechanical aids (glue, etc.).

The snails were made from strips of paper, the insect was developed out of the rectangle, the swan out of a specially cut sheet.

Figures 251-61: here, the basic form is the tube (cylinder). First of all, a certain number of tubes must be made (narrow, wide, pointed, funnel-shaped, etc.). The most suitable material is thin drawing paper, rolled round a pencil or pen-holder and stuck together at the edges

252 M 13

253 J 12

255 M 15

254 J 13

256 J 13

88

257 J 15

The tubes are then joined. In the case of the animals illustrated here, the students were allowed to make further cuts, insertions and creases, etc.

Figures 258-61: these animals are movable and can change their expressions quite easily. Children could make a whole farmyard together

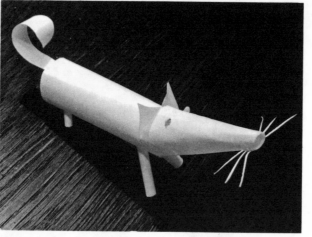

258 M 15

259 J 12

260 J 15

261

262 M 15

263 V

264 M 15

265 V

The trees shown on pages 91 and 92 were made in different ways. The simplest way is to roll up a rectangle (or triangle) which has been cut into like a comb along its base. The strips will curl if pressed quickly with the back of a knife

Figure 264: rings of various sizes, cut into at the edges and slid over a cone

Figure 265: a tube, with leaves stuck into it

The reader can discover the stages of figure 267 for himself

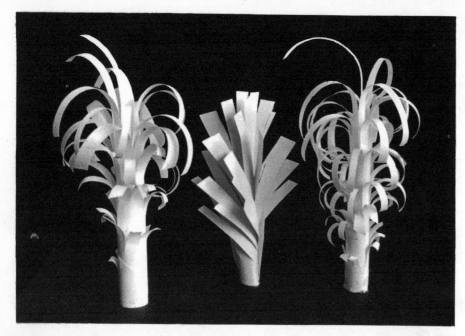

266 J + M 11

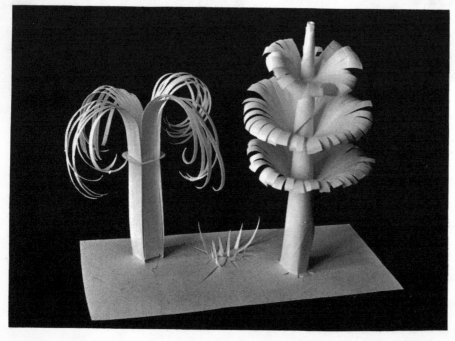

267 V

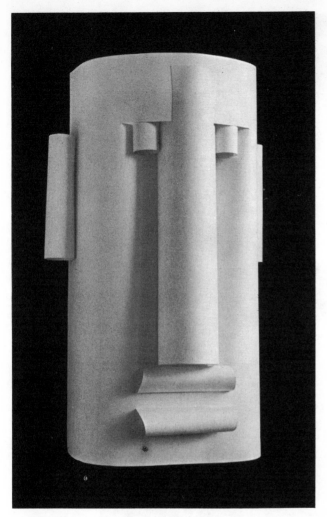

268 J 13

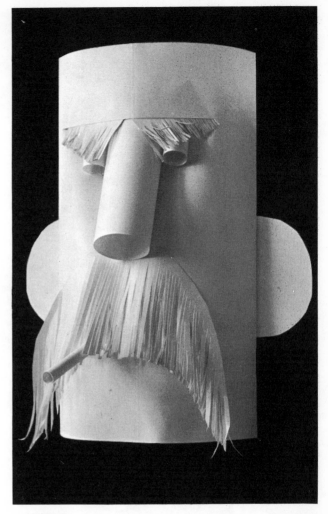

269 J 13

Making faces from paper is a rewarding task.

Figures 268-9: a sheet of drawing paper was curved to form a half-cylinder like a vault. The rules demanded that all the forms used for eyes, ears, nose and mouth should be related to the cylinder or the circle, although extra eyebrows and beard and moustache were permitted

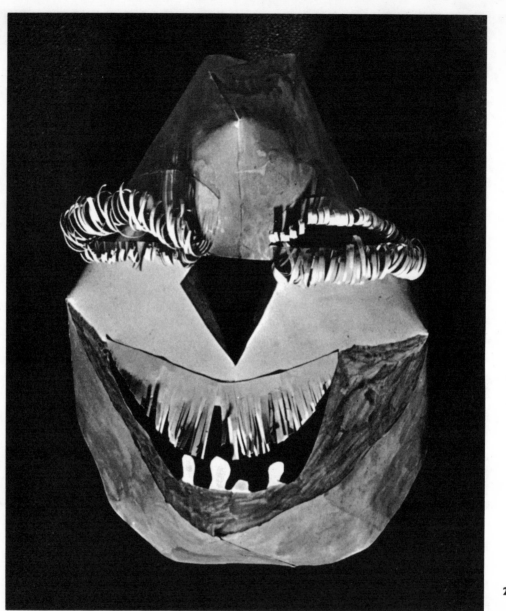

270 J 14

A mask made by cutting in and folding out. Care must be taken when using water colours, because damp easily makes the paper soft. Pasting on pieces of coloured paper is more appropriate to the material and strengthens the form

94

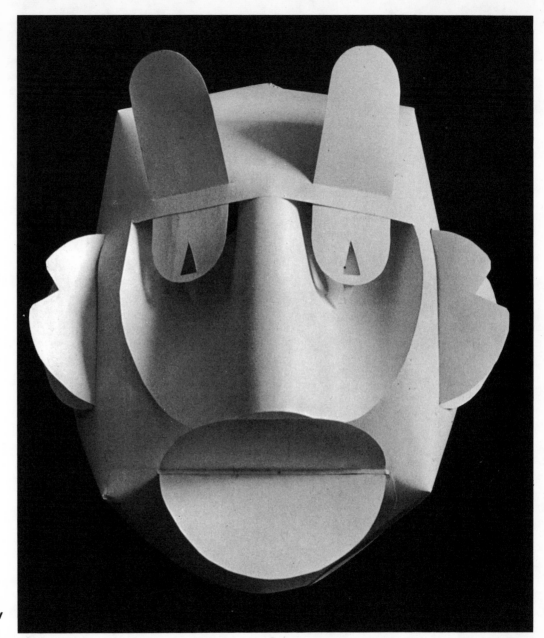

271 V

The work of an advanced student, achieved entirely through bending, cutting into and inserting. No glue or paste has been used